GRACE

GRACE

Building Wealth—One Penny at a Time

Calvin C. Barlow Jr.

LOWBAR
PUBLISHING COMPANY
NASHVILLE

CALVIN C. BARLOW JR., AUTHOR

Printed in the United States of America in 2011
© 2011 by Lowbar Publishing Company

ISBN: **978-0-9827151-4-7**
Lowbar Publishing Company
Nashville, Tennessee 37204
615-972-2842
E-mail: Lowbar@comcast.net
Web site: www.Lowbarbookstore.com

Editor/Copy Editor: Tanae C. McKnight Murdic
Layout Designer: Sharon Hardin
Graphic Art and Book Cover Designer: Sharon Hardin

For speaking engagements, workshops, and seminars, here is how you may contact the author:

Lowbar Publishing Company
905 South Douglas Avenue
Nashville, TN 37204
Phone: (615) 972-2842
Lowbar@comcast.net

ॐ

My sincere appreciation is extended to Ms. Florence Jean Wright, a woman in her seventies who moves as a twenty-year-old sprinter and has the beauty and charm of an eighteen-year-old prom queen. God used this woman of faith to sow into my spiritual being the unrealized power of a penny. This sowing impregnated my thoughts to give birth to the book, *Grace*.

ॐ

Contents

Preface

Those who purchase this book and adhere to its principles will be blessed financially. *Grace* will inspire readers to change their lifestyles, or it will affirm that their lifestyles are in harmony with the biblical principles that they must apply to gain wealth. God makes available to every Christian the tools to be utilized in gaining wealth. In other words, each Christian can live an abundant life when these biblical principles are activated. Possessing wealth does not mean that each person has the same quantity as another, but that each person has an amount that exceeds personal needs.

God expects Christians to be blessings to others. Mission fields require physical labor and funds. God expects Christians to give to the poor, and for Christians to honor Him with their earthly substances. These objectives cannot be achieved without the building of wealth among the body of Christ. Moreover, God does not expect sinners to support kingdom work. Thus, those who adhere to the principles of biblical wealth building will not be slaves to fund-raisers as the only means of supporting church ministries.

Finally, those who purchase this book will recover its cost within ten days. If the principles of the book are put into action, then the purchaser will have saved $5.12 in ten days, and $40.96 in thirteen days. Thus, the principles learned from the models presented in this book will transform and revolutionize the reader's lifestyle in every arena of life.

Acknowledgments

It is not often that the teachings of a coach reverberate beyond the realm of the grave. However, this is the case with my deceased father, Calvin Coolidge Barlow Sr., my mentor and hero. He taught his family, by example, how to appreciate the splendor of earth without getting caught up in man's glitter. He showed us how to use character and integrity to build wealth. If I have any regrets in this life, they would be that my father did not live to see the publication of this book, and that my mother did not live to see me receive my Master's degree. I am eternally grateful to my mother, Annie Katherine Barlow, my greatest supporter and cheerleader—and Calvin Coolidge Barlow Sr., a faithful husband and devoted father. They raised fourteen children with pennies, in comparison to today's incomes. They did not have much, but what they did have they lavished it in love. Finally, I thank my deceased grandfather, John Barlow—a man of wisdom—who once said to us, "It's not how much money you have, but it's how you use the money that you have." Thus, *Grace* is a reflection of my childhood memories, blended with research, personal experience, and observation.

INTRODUCTION

When was the last time that you looked at a penny and saw more than a penny? When was the last time you ignored your pride and picked up a penny? Is it not strange that we would break our necks to pick up a twenty-dollar bill, yet walk past a penny? It is unfortunate that we live in a time when the penny has lost its value. However, true and lasting wealth is built one day (and one penny) at a time—and it requires discipline and a systematic plan.

Everything in life starts with one. God is one (see Deuteronomy 6:4). One God created the one earth—and the universe and all of its glory. The one God created the one man and the one woman. God brought the one man and the one woman together in holy matrimony, and of this union the one family was produced—the human family, with all of its diversity—which is the human race (see Genesis 2:22-24). From one body of water flow all oceans, rivers, lakes, creeks, ponds, and springs. It rains because of the mystery of the one body of water (see Genesis 1:7). Ice, sleet, hail, and snow get their power from the source of the one body of water.

Furthermore, without the one God's creation, there would be no universe, galaxy, or planets to discover (neither would there be a big bang to bang without the creation of that which was needed for the banging). The birds would not soar above the earth. There would be no wiggling snakes moving to the rhythm of earth's cadence. There would be no continents or nations. There would be no tribes, or languages, or differently hued persons—had it not been for the one God. ONE is the source and origin of all good and bad. However, most people never see one cent, one penny, as being the original source of millions upon billions of dollars in our monetary system.

You cannot have two cars until you have had one car. You cannot have two houses until you have had one house. You cannot have one dollar until you have had one cent (one penny). Now you can dream all day about having two houses, but until you get the first house, you will never have the second house. Yet, this is what some people do when it comes to creating wealth: they dream about millions of dollars while casting aside the millions of pennies.

Perhaps what defeats us in our quest to achieve the achievable is the delusion of the mind as it summarizes quantities. For example, some people see the mega churches as a status of religionist elitism or the ultimate pastoral success, while failing to see that no congregation starts with one thousand, two thousand, or twenty thousand members. Every congregation starts small. Consequently, when it comes to developing personal wealth, the mind sees and seeks to model the mega, the much, the great. The mind sees the joy on the faces of those who attend the mega affairs of life. The mind sees the flashing neon lights, the billboards, the Benzes, the giveaways, and the brochures of the mega, the much, the great. Unfortunately, the mind does not see the struggles, the dedication, the consistency, and the attention given to the least before the mega achieved its mega status. Thus, some people walk past pennies in the hopes of finding something greater.

Stop and think: how many pennies have you walked right past, while you would have made the effort to stop and pick up a dollar? Moreover, had it been a "C note," you would have put some pep in your step. Nevertheless, because the penny did not have a present value for your current reality, you walked past it and disregarded its potential for greatness. This is how some people live their lives. They never develop their potentials—as they seem too small and irrelevant. Thus, they live lives of walking past their potentials while fraternizing with other people's greatness on borrowed money and borrowed time.

For example, taking a vacation or a cruise that you could not afford may have given you momentary joy among your peers—however, it was joy built on a quicksand reality. Now, there is not anything wrong with taking a vacation or a cruise, but doing so should never undermine your potential. The Bible teaches that the borrower is a slave to the lender (see Proverbs 22:7). Thus, when we borrow from our futures, we make ourselves slaves to our yesterdays.

In real time, this is a bill. For example, the shoes that you could not leave on the shoe rack; the new game that you just had to have though you had not mastered the last two games you purchased. Now, the bill is due—but Aunt Mary just died and you need to purchase a set of car tires to make the trip. When we rob our futures, we are not prepared to take care of the present. Consequently, many people live lives to where the actions enacted on their yesterdays keep them in slavery. However, when we allow God the opportunity to develop our potentials, He always provides for our present and future needs. Thus, when we attribute value to the penny, we gain the mindsets that help us to trust that God can always provide dollars for our future needs.

The intent of the book is to help its readers find joy in becoming great rather than faking greatness. The lesson to be learned from the book is that wealth is a measurement of what is earned, what is saved, and what is spent. The process of acquiring wealth is likened unto the penny's requiring a continual gathering, discipline, focus, commitment, and dedication in order to become a dollar. After reading this book, persons should begin to create financial stability by making healthy lifestyle choices. Finally, the book has charts in chapter 6 that demonstrate the power of the penny in obtaining wealth.

DISCUSSION QUESTIONS

1. Why do most people find it easier to fake greatness rather than achieve greatness?

2. What stops people from realizing that borrowing is a type of robbery?

3. In your opinion, what prevents most people from picking up a penny?

1

BUILDING A LEGACY WITH PENNIES

Jesus looked up and saw some rich people tossing their gifts into the offering box. He also saw a poor widow putting in two pennies. And he said, "I tell you that this poor woman has put in more than all the others."—Luke 21:1-3 (CEV)

Some years ago, Second Missionary Baptist Church's church school decided to challenge the youth to save pennies for a "Penny Rally." The child who saved and turned in the most pennies received a trophy and a cash prize. To my amazement, the parents gave of themselves in helping their children to collect pennies. And those children without parents attending the congregation were mentored by other members, who helped them gather pennies.

As I reflect upon twenty-six years of pastoral ministry, the Penny Rally holds first place in my mind. Even though a new sanctuary, an educational wing, and many ministries have been added, over the years, the Penny Rally built character in those potential leaders. The church's primary job is to offer Christ as the Savior of the world and to help build character in those who accept Him as Savior. These children were given the opportunity to develop their potentials. Thus, the Penny Rally shaped their minds in order to positively affect their dispositions for the future.

This is what takes place when an individual gathers one penny at a time:

- He or she learns to give proper attention to the small things in life.

- He or she learns that there is a common denominator in the process of acquiring the larger things in life.

- He or she learns that preparation for his or her success sets the stage for his or her recognizing that success.

- He or she learns that small things *do* matter.

- He or she learns that dollars stand on the shoulders of pennies.

- He or she learns how to prevent pride from robbing him or her of his or her potential.

The children who participated in the Penny Rally learned that adulthood is built on and shaped by the actions of childhood. Twenty-six years later, all of the children who participated in the Penny Rally are tithers of the church—with the exception of a few.

In actuality, the woman in the Luke 21 Scripture passage gave two coins that had a value totaling less than a penny in our currency. The coins she gave were called *mites* and represented the least amount in monetary value during Jesus' time (according to the Jewish monetary system).

The Bible says that Jesus showed up at church and decided to stand next to the offering plates. From study of the text, it is obvious that Christ has showed up to observe one's application of the Law—as he or she has knowledge of the Law. The truth is that most people have knowledge of God's Word but an inability to apply it to their lives.

It is possible that the widow had more than two coins, initially. However, when she arrived at the Temple, she only had two coins. Thus, she placed all that she had in the treasury of God. Thus, she did not allow her lack of funds to stop her from honoring the law of God. In other words, she did not reason within herself that the rent had to be paid. She did not reason within herself that the grandchildren might need school clothing. This widow honored God according to her faith in the law of God. She honored God by obeying truth, despite her monetary deficiency. The church would do well to emulate this widow, because the Bible says that obedience is better than sacrifice (see 1 Samuel 15:22).

Furthermore, it has to be assumed that the widow was truly disciplined. A person who is disciplined does not deviate from the rules. In other words, a disciplined person trains him- or herself to obey the rules. This is why Paul challenged young Timothy to study the Word (see 2 Timothy 2:14). The studying of God's Word helps us to obey God's rules—His standards. Finally, the widow was blessed monetarily because of her faithfulness and obedience to God's precepts and commandments.

> "Bring the whole tithe into the storehouse, that there may be food in my house. Test me in this," says the Lord Almighty, "and see if I will not throw open the floodgates of heaven and pour out so much blessing that you will not have enough room for it" (Malachi 3:10, NIV).

> "Give, and it will be given to you. A good measure, pressed down, shaken together and running over, will be poured into your lap. For with the measure you use, it will be measured to you" (Luke 6:38, NIV).

A man died at the age of eighty-five, after having raised fourteen children and with approximately eighty-five-hundred dollars in his bank account. This man was able to send to college all of his children who were eager to achieve that level of education. He accomplished all of this on a salary of three hundred dollars per week. After he retired, he managed to keep in his checking account a balance of more than one thousand dollars per month, on an income of seven hundred per month. When he died, his house was paid for, and he had no outstanding bills. Upon his death, the funds that he had accumulated were enough to pay for his burial—after which he had some left over for his daughters. His estate gave a final tithe to the church of five hundred dollars. This man, like the widow in the Scripture text, honored God with his pennies. My recollections of him focus on how he was able to manage pennies to achieve integrity and nobility. This man was my father. At this factory worker's funeral, the mayor of the city gave remarks that spoke to his work ethics and moral and family values. I would like to believe that honor was bestowed upon this humble servant because he paid proper attention to the small things in life.

Most of us have heard the saying, "It is the small things that matter in life." Yet, most people fail to apply this truth when given the opportunity. The widow took advantage of her opportunity: she gave her pennies; she placed her trust in the Lord's treasury—and her fame is linked to the least, not the most.

The content of the text supports God's desire for us to give our best to Him. Like Abel of the Old Testament, the widow gave God her best. Her pennies did not have the same monetary value as the rich people's offerings, but she gave her best. In her society, she did not receive the same recognition as the rich people. Yet, she did not allow others to intimidate her into not giving of her best.

What is your best? Your best might be a twenty-dollar bill, while for your group it is a "C note." Be proud of your twenty! If you offer your best to glorify God, then God will glorify you. However, keep in mind that your twenty stands on the shoulders of the penny. Therefore, do not walk past the penny because you have a twenty—the penny represents your potential.

The widow's story helps us understand the power and potential for greatness in the small things (or the least of things). In other words, we learn from the story that greatness is embedded in the least. This principle is seen in nature, when we plant a kernel of corn in order to harvest ears of corn. Therefore, the next time you see a penny, do not walk past it. Pick it up, give it to a child, and help him or her to understand the potential of wealth hidden in the penny.

In conclusion, the widow did as was required of the man in the story of the "talents": she made an investment in the marketplace (see Matthew 25:27). Every time we give to God's kingdom on earth—which is the church—we are making an investment in the marketplace of life. The widow did not see her gift as being too small or insignificant to produce a greater outcome. Yet, too many people see the penny as being too small or insignificant to produce the greater outcome of personal wealth.

The belief that a penny is too small to affect one's personal wealth creates a defeatist attitude that perpetuates poverty for those who have the least in life. Thus, persons of this mindset live lives characterized by the borrowing and consumption of things that are wants rather than needs. Therefore, every person or family should seek to live in a way that reflects spending in relation to his or her saving and income. So when a family's spending prevents the family from saving, the family cannot sustain itself. Consequently, for many families, the lack of income is not the problem—the problem stems from the inability to manage earned income in a manner that creates sustainability. Thus, the widow in the Scripture text demonstrated that a properly managed income affords an individual the opportunity to honor moral obligations. Giving to God's kingdom is a moral obligation of every Christian.

DISCUSSION QUESTIONS

1. Why is honoring God with our earthly possessions a moral obligation?

2. What does nature teach us about greatness?

3. Why is obedience better than sacrifice?

2

THE VALUE OF A PENNY

It appears that our twenty-first-century society has lost its admiration for the penny. Nobody brags about having a common penny. We leave pennies in unused purses. We cast them aside in places not to be found. Some wishing wells even frown upon the penny. Some stores give them to their customers to round off their purchases. Even the scrap value of a penny's copper does not have the same value as silver. In other words, in a world of "wannabes," the penny is nobody.

However, there was a time when the penny was sought after for its purchasing power:

- When one penny could buy two pieces of bubble gum

- When one penny could buy you two small cookies

- When five pennies could buy you two pieces of rag bologna and two crackers

- When one hundred pennies gave status to a poor boy

Those were the days of the penny in the 1940s, 1950s, and early 1960s. Those days are gone. In this day, there are those who believe that the production cost of the penny outweighs its value.

According to a 1923 Sears Roebuck Catalog, you could buy the following items at these prices:

- A work shirt for eighty-nine cents

- A leather coin purse for twenty-one cents

- A pair of leather shoes for $1.79

- A sports hat for sixty-five cents

- A necktie for twenty-five cents

- A dress shirt for one dollar

- A smoking pipe for seventy-five cents

- A bride-and-groom wedding-ring set (18K white gold) for ten dollars

In the early 1900s, people did not walk past a penny. However, the penny has the same potential for wealth building today as it did many years ago.

The penny is valuable to those who understand the monetary system of the United States of America. The penny is a percentage of a dollar. The dollar is a percentage of a one-hundred-dollar bill. A one-hundred-dollar bill is a percentage of a one-thousand-dollar bill. Thus, if there are approximately 304 million people in America and each person was given five pennies per day—for 365 days—then the amount from this scenario would total $5,548,000,000. This figure is the reason why most retailers do not give pennies away. Oil companies understand the power of a penny. According to the *Seattle Times*, "Americans used 8.93 million barrels of gasoline a day in 2003. A barrel holds 42 gallons; that is roughly 375 million gallons per day" *(Ask.Yahoo.com)*. Therefore, taking into account the above statistic, when oil companies raise the cost of a gallon of gas by one cent, the revenue of oil companies is increased approximately $1,368,000,000 per year. Unfortunately, the average person does not appreciate the value of a penny.

Most employers raise the salaries of their employees by cents and not dollars. The employer who has a labor force of a thousand people and gives each employee a five-cent raise per hour pays out approximately an extra $104,000 per year on those five cents alone. However, the employee will not see a significant increase in take-home pay. Assuming a forty-hour workweek, the increase only amounts to $2 per week (or $104 per year)—most of which will be absorbed by taxes. Therefore, a penny does not have the same value for an employee as it does for an employer. Thus, this is the disconnection for most persons. The value of the penny is tied to present value and not potential worth.

It is believed that the average person will drop about 1400 pennies in a lifetime. This means that on the average, Americans as a whole will throw away approximately $4,256,000,000 in a lifetime. Assuming that a lifetime is 69 years, approximately $61 million goes unclaimed in pennies every year. Thus, when you pass by a penny, you are passing by potentially thousands of dollars. Here is a bit of background history on the penny (paraphrased):

> Originally, the coin was larger and made of pure copper. In 1857, the penny was made up of 88 percent copper and 12 percent nickel. The penny today has a composition of about 97.5 percent zinc and 2.5 percent copper. (www.usmint.gov)

The value of the penny lies in its gathering. While more pennies—as a group—are required in order for them to have real purchasing power today, the outcome is the same. Building wealth is a process that requires consistency in, discipline for, and dedication to the effort.

DISCUSSION QUESTIONS

1. Why do large corporations value pennies?

2. Why do most employees fail to give value to the penny?

3. How many dollars have you walked past (in pennies)?

3

PENNY TALK

Learned skills are portable and transferrable. In other words, most skills are based upon principles and are related to the laws of science, mathematics, nature, and other factors. For example, if you learn how to bake a cake, then the same skills learned—such as how to read a measuring cup, or knowing the difference between a teaspoon and tablespoon—can be useful for baking bread or making a chemical formula. Therefore, the time, consistency, and discipline applied to gathering a penny are aspects of the process applicable to other arenas in life.

In chapter 6, you will find charts that provide clear illustrations of the power of a penny, and how an individual may come to engage in wealth building on the premise of this power. These charts will help you to integrate your savings from other sources. Furthermore, you will see where you stand financially, as you seek to build wealth that is biblically based. However, the question remains: what value does the gathering of pennies teach that possessing a twenty- or fifty-dollar bill could not teach?

Appreciation and Respect

In society, appreciation and respect are linked to value. In other words, if an object or person is considered valuable, then it/he/she receives respect and appreciation. So, in dealing with money, the twenty- or fifty-dollar bill is what is given value, because it has an immediate purchasing power—whereas the penny does not. But merely giving a person a twenty- or fifty-dollar bill does little to develop within that individual a true appreciation for wealth building. This appreciation could stem from a person's being consistent in gathering pennies in order for the pennies to reach their purchasing power. Thus, consistency is one of the building blocks for acquiring wealth. Additionally, those who achieve wealth have learned to pay close attention to details and the little things in life.

People would benefit from learning the societal value in gathering pennies, which cannot be learned effectively from possessing a twenty- or fifty-dollar bill. Too often, we base people's worth on their present status, not their potential. Having a regular penny in your pocket does not carry the same status as having a fifty-dollar bill in your pocket. Thus, we will pass by those persons or objects that do not exude position and status in life. For example, the boy (penny) who is from the east side of the tracks does not receive the same fairness as the boy (twenty- or fifty-dollar bill) from the west side of the tracks in the judicial system because his parents are pennies. In other words, there is a lack of respect and appreciation for the boy based upon his surface value. However, those who gather pennies should be able to see value in persons based upon potential and not present value.

Commitment and Discipline

To commit is to obligate or to bind oneself to a purpose or goal. In other words, one takes a pledge to achieve an objective. Incidentally, wealth cannot be achieved without commitment. Therefore, if one decided that he or she wants fifty dollars, but has to gather pennies in order to obtain it, then he or she would have to be committed in order to achieve the desired objective. And if a person demonstrates commitment in one facet of life, then it is possible for that same principle to be applied in other facets of life.

Empowerment and Enabling

To *empower* a person is to give or share authority with that individual. To *enable* a person is to provide that person with the opportunity or the means to accomplish something or to reach for a goal. In other words, if a person shares his or her authority with you, then he or she is *empowering* you. However, if the same person places you in a position to attain authority, then he or she is *enabling* you. While both empowerment and enablement are necessary for wealth building, enablement has a lasting effect. For example, many persons were empowered as the result of the Civil Rights movement. However, many discovered some years later that authority given could be authority taken away. Therefore, empowerment should only be used to jump-start the wealth-building process—not used as the means to the end of the process.

The gathering of pennies is an act of empowerment *and* enablement. For example, if you have the goal of raising fifty dollars, and a person gives you one hundred pennies, then this act could be considered an act of empowerment. On the other hand, it could be an act of enablement, because it places you in the position to achieve the desired goal. Thus, you can begin to realize that most wealthy people are empowered people who have become enabled people. Therefore, the gathering of pennies is not the end of the means but, rather, the beginning of the means to gaining wealth. The penny model helps us to see that wealth is a building process that requires continual gathering and discipline. Gathering pennies is not an easy assignment—but if you are able to master the technique, then the behavior skills learned can be applied to other areas in your life.

Lifestyle

How an individual chooses to live will determine that person's opportunity to gain wealth. It is true that most people do not have a wealth problem, but most people have a lifestyle problem. In other words, if wealth can be seen as one's having more than he or she needs, then an unrealistic lifestyle will always seek to satisfy wants and not needs. For example, a person who makes $800 per week can buy a car, and pay $800 per month for the car payment. However, the car payment will most likely diminish the potential to build wealth. Yet, a person who makes $1800 per week should be able to afford a car payment of $800 per month without diminishing the potential to build wealth. If wealth building is the desired goal, then a person's expenses should not exceed 75 percent of income. Thus, this is the question that an individual must ask him- or herself: "What can I afford?"—not, "What can I buy?" Just because you can purchase something does not mean that you can *afford* it.

The housing crisis of 2008 is a prime example of people's buying what they could not afford. Many people purchased houses on their buying ability and not affordability. For example, if it takes two incomes to qualify for a house, then the house is not affordable. Just because someone makes it easy for you to buy something does not mean that you can afford the item. Thus, buying on credit is only as good as the borrower's ability to liquidate credit at any moment. A payment of credit based upon the borrower's unearned income can potentially place him or her in default crisis. Credit purchases should be made upon liquidation principles to protect wealth building. In other words, whatever is purchased by credit must have the ability to be liquidated without disrupting wealth-building outcomes. One's effort of gathering pennies helps him or her to realize that an individual cannot live like a dollar when he or she is just a penny.

Debt robs a person of purchasing power. In other words, if your paycheck is $2000 and you owe $1500, then you only have $500 worth of purchasing power. When you use credit cards to purchase items, for which the cost you cannot liquidate in twenty-five to thirty days, you end up paying two to three times the cost of the items you would have spent (had you paid cash)—especially if you pay the minimum amount required to be in good standing. Gathering pennies is not easy, nor is building wealth. However, the gathering of pennies teaches that there are some things that need to be placed on hold until they can be afforded. The challenge for most people lies in resisting the desire to live like a dollar on penny ability.

Prophetic Insight

The ability to see the end at the beginning is the definition of the gift of prophecy. The prophets spoke of the outcome before the realization of the outcome. Thus, the person who gathers pennies must be able to "see" dollars as they gather pennies. Therefore, the person who seeks to build wealth would do well to be able to predict future outcomes while standing in the present.

One's commitment to that which is not seen (before it is realized) demands conviction on his or her part. Thus, most people who desire to be wealthy never become wealthy—because they never reach a level of true conviction. When a person is convicted of an idea, the idea dominates his or her life. In other words, the goal becomes the objective and the objective becomes the priority until the goal is reached. In layman's terms, getting a job cannot be the goal for those who seek to build wealth—wealth building has to be the *reason* for seeking the job.

Finally, the person who gathers pennies does so knowing that enough wrapped pennies equal dollars. The behavior implementation for this discipline is one of consistency, commitment, and dedication. This theory is an observational fact. Thus, the model of gathering pennies teaches wealth seekers that wealth building is a theory based upon observational facts. Even though a person's insight may lead him or her down a road of unknowns, the end of the journey is assured, based upon observational facts.

DISCUSSION QUESTIONS

1. What is the difference between *empowerment* and *enablement*?

2. What skill sets are learned from gathering pennies?

3. What effect does a person's lifestyle choice have on his or her ability to build wealth?

4

THE FALLACY OF ACTING WEALTHY

Have you seen those persons who act wealthy but are living from one paycheck to another? Persons who live this type of lifestyle participate in activities in which they cannot afford to indulge. And before you say "That is not me," the truth is that *most* people face this reality. A tax advisor made a statement that she had many doctor and lawyer friends who were struggling financially because they could not handle their finances. Now, most people would find it unimaginable to believe that a doctor or a high-priced attorney would be struggling to pay a mortgage note. Recently, one of Michael Jackson's doctors—who portrayed a lavish lifestyle to the public—was, for all intent and purpose, broke. In other words, most people have tried to maintain lifestyles with which they cannot keep up.

The Bible teaches that there is a season for everything (see Ecclesiastes 3:1). Yet, most of us find it difficult to wait for our season—and it is because of this impatience that many people suffer from the "Jones's Syndrome." The *Jones's Syndrome* is characterized by a need to "represent." Most people are aware of their need to be loved and appreciated, but few people realize that we also have a need to feel that we have accomplished something or that we have "arrived." While a myriad of books has been written to help us deal with low self-esteem—due to a love or appreciation deficit—few (if any) books have been written that help us to deal with the need to feel that we have "arrived." Thus, this basic need of most rational people goes unattended, eventually wreaking havoc in the lives of its victims.

For example, many people attend conventions and seminars and stay in hotels at prices that they cannot afford. A story was shared with me about a pastor who attended conventions year after year on his personal funds just to be seen among his peers. The truth is that many persons wrestle, as does this pastor, with the need to feel a sense of accomplishment among peers—at the expense of wreaking havoc on their personal lives.

There are several reasons why an individual may be on a quest to feel accomplished:

> **YOU ONLY LIVE ONCE**. Theory dictates that you must enjoy this life at any cost (while you can) and should not plan for tomorrow—for it might not come. The fallacy of the theory lies in the question, "What if you live longer than expected?" It is one thing to be working at the local grocery store, sacking groceries for health reasons, but it is quite another thing to work there in order to pay the water bill.

A significant number of people do not have enough income to sustain them in their retirement years. According to recent data, the average American saves $397 in a savings account per year. The average nest egg for a person who retires between the ages of 65 and 75 is approximately $56,000, according to the Employee Benefit Research Institute (www.bargaineering.com). Therefore, it is delusional to think that you can live a lifestyle of youthful recklessness and not diminish the quality of your "golden years."

> **LOSS OF INCOME.** I can recall an instance in a real-estate class when the instructor asked the students to look at a specific case study and qualify the buyer to purchase a house.

The case study gave a couple of options to make the qualification possible:

• Sell the new car and take the cash to buy a used, yet dependable car.

• Cancel the family insurance, because the couple was under the age of forty with a baby, and reinstating the policy would not cost more in two years.

Many of the students suggested that the family insurance should be cancelled and that the new car should be kept. If repairs were not the problem, then what could have possibly influenced the students to make such a fatal decision? Thus, it had to be that the new car represented status—a feeling of accomplishment. Consequently, this is the same reason why many families fail to downsize their lifestyles when they have a loss of income in the family. Many families struggle financially, not because they are bad stewards, but because they do not have the willpower to give up lifestyles that they can no longer afford to maintain. Consequently, this weakness sows the seed of havoc in their lives, thus robbing them of serenity in their golden years.

Persons who live fallacious lifestyles, regardless of the reason, will always live lives of uncertainty. While it is true that death and taxes are guarantees in this life, it is also true that persons are capable of living lives of wealth. Thus, a person needs to find a model that builds wealth for the least of society. Building wealth via a penny is an achievable goal, and the model is accessible to every person who desires to live an abundant life.

➢ **DO NOT LEAVE IT FOR FOLKS TO FIGHT OVER.** This is a selfish theory. It dictates that *for the sake of denying others, I will spend it all on my wants and not needs.* Its primary purpose is to deny children their inheritance and to make sure that funds are not left to serve a greater purpose for humanity.

The theory is applicable to the story of the rich young ruler. He refused to give his possessions to the poor so that he might follow Jesus. When a person would rather spend his or her funds on wants rather than to give it to the poor, he or she is disobeying the Word of God. The Bible admonishes Christians to give to the poor (see Proverbs 19:17).

Usually, persons with these characteristics—if they are church members—are the worst members. They complain the most yet give the least money and time. They are growth killers. They will not give and they will call other members and tell them why they should not give as well. Out in the world, these people spend their weekends in casinos and refuse to give one dollar to charitable organizations. However, these persons are guilty of living misleading lifestyles. Unfortunately, these groups of people are envied by some believers. When you are giving your tithes and being accountable to God with your talents, you may ask the question, "God, how can these people cruise on Your money, shop on Your time, and still live fashionable lives?" This is why God's Word says, "Fret not thyself over evildoers" (see Psalm 37:1). God does not bless us to be blessings for ourselves but blessings to others.

Again, the word *wealth* denotes quantitativeness, meaning that it can be measured. This does not mean that each person will have the same things. For example, if an individual must have one hundred dollars in order to be considered wealthy, yet only has seventy-five dollars, then he or she is considered poor. However, in the real world, the person who has seventy-five dollars is just as wealthy as the person who has a hundred dollars—if that person's lifestyle only consumes fifty dollars of the seventy-five dollars. To have wealth is to have more than you need. Thus, the definition of practical wealth challenges our lifestyles' preference for consumer goods. Do you really need two Porsches and a Bentley? Do you really need to wear designer clothing to be clothed? Consequently, some people who make millions of dollars are broke, laden with tax debts or stuck in a federal penitentiary because of unhealthy lifestyle preferences. In contrast, there is the person who tithes and gives regularly to charitable organizations that has a healthy savings account, a comfortable home, and a decent car or two.

Wealth is the amount of disposable income that a person has after meeting moral and legal obligations. For example, a financial planner would look at a person's total assets and liabilities and declare the person as either wealthy or broke. However, assets must be measured by a liquidity test. In other words, not all assets have the same liquidity. Liquidity considers conversion, time, and marketability. A house is an asset, but its cash value is linked to time and demand. Stocks and bonds are assets, but they are linked to the vulnerability of a global marketplace. Fixed assets are the only assets that have real cash value, such as savings accounts, certificates of deposit, government bonds, and money-market accounts. However, fixed assets yield the least amount of interest on invested dollars.

It would be safe to say that a large percentage of America's families are acting as though they are wealthy. Thus, they are living misleading or deceptive lifestyles. In other words, they are buying what they cannot afford and spending money that does not belong to them. They are driving, shopping, and cruising on unrealized income. The fallacy of acting wealthy is that you spend what you do not have to impress others or to obtain a momentary social high. Be reminded that just because you have a "C note" in your pocket does not mean that it is spendable.

DISCUSSION QUESTIONS

1. How should wealth be defined?

2. Why should assets be measured by a liquidity test?

3. What are some of the causes that lead people to live lifestyles that they cannot afford?

5

TEACHING A NEW GENERATION HOW TO BUILD WEALTH

When I was a child, my father introduced me to gardening. Whereas my brothers disliked manual labor, it was a love for me. There was something mystical about the process of planting a garden. I loved the smell of the soil. I loved to till the soil. I loved to watch the seeds grow into plants, and the plants produce their fruit.

The opening of the topsoil exposed another world to me. Beneath the topsoil was a sub-terrestrial world where earthworms built their habitat. It was where ants carved out their tunnels to store food for the winter. I discovered that earth mammals, snakes, moles, and many creatures of God lived just beneath the topsoil. The removal of the topsoil exposed another world. Likewise, wealth-building techniques allow children the opportunity to explore the possibilities and workings of a global financial system underneath the veil of their imaginations. My exposure to gardening has had a direct influence on my ability and excitement to grow businesses. There is the same effect when children are exposed to the process of gathering pennies. The more pennies they gather, the more money they have to take to the bank—and this increases their excitement level. In many instances, children would never experience the workings of a bank until they reached eighteen years of age or older.

We send our children to school to learn skill sets for life. We encourage our children to participate in sports in order to learn discipline and structure. However, too many parents fail to teach their children how to manage money and build wealth. The Hebrew writer taught us to train up a child so that he or she knows what to do (see Proverbs 22:6). So, this is the question we must ask: "How do we train our children to build wealth?" Thus, purpose should always precede methodology. It is a fact that as humanity progresses, so does the evil and selfishness of humanity. Consequently, the child who reaches age 20 in 2025 will exist in a world that is bankrupt of moral values and compassion for the poor. Thus, it is imperative that those who love God be able to create jobs, rather than having to tolerate the slave wages of ungodly corporations.

As we approach the next decade, we are witnesses to the attacks of the rich, ungodly corporations and "bought" government officials—elected and appointed—attacking the upward mobility of the middle class and the poor. There is an effort by the politicians (mostly Republicans in the twenty-first century) to roll back every gain that the poor have obtained since the late 1960s. Without a quality education and a good job, or the ability to create a job, people are forced to take crumbs from an elite group of people that makes up less than 15 percent of America's population. According to recent data (www.mybudget360.com), the top 1 percent controls approximately 42 percent of America's wealth.

When the spokesperson of the "Heritage Foundation," the Rush Limbaughs, and the Shawn Hannitys of the twenty-first century can imply that a person is not poor because he or she has a "we tote your note" car parked on the grass and a pawn shop plasma TV on their living-room walls, we are living in stupid town. These persons are doing everything they can do to take away the advantages of the middle-income families and poor families. When a person has to make a decision between food and medicine, he or she is poor. An individual who has to suffer inhumane treatment—whether voluntarily or involuntarily—is robbed of his or her dignity and worth. When a group or a person is not able to determine its/his/her destiny, for all intent and purpose, the group or person is a slave. However, God did not call Christians to be slaves to a world of greedy tyrants—but a slave to *Him*. Therefore, it is imperative that we teach children (especially Christian children) how to build wealth—and the church needs to participate in the educational process.

Most church members hear preachers saying that God owns the cattle on thousands of hills, and that the silver and gold belong to Him. They hear the Scripture that reads, "The earth is the LORD's, and the fulness thereof" (Psalm 24:1, KJV). All of these are true statements, and we would be delusional to believe that God has not made available a system whereby the saints of God could discover these earthly benefits. In other words, in a free society, we have not the things of God because we fail to place God's Word into action, and to be consistent in our efforts.

Even though God's earthly principles work for the unsaved, the principles are outlined for the children of God. Thus, there are too many parents who do not require that their children save a tithe for the Lord's house. If a child is not taught to support the Lord's house, then he or she will not respect his or her house. Tithing teaches a child to value money. Tithing teaches a child that some things come *first*. Tithing teaches a child that an earned dollar is not always a spendable dollar. Finally, tithing teaches a child how to save that which is earned for another day. Tithing is the first step in teaching a Christian child some wealth-building techniques.

Too many Christians fail to teach their children how to manage money in a manner that builds wealth. Instead of taking our children to the bank to establish a savings account or to the library to acquire knowledge, we take them to the water parks and the shopping malls. It is at the shopping mall that children learn how to spend money on things that they cannot afford to buy and do not need. It is at the water park that children learn how to have fun with other people's money.

There is a need to go to school, but meeting this need requires work. The library offers a child a wealth of knowledge and a glimpse into worlds yet unvisited; these discoveries help shape the character and behavior of a child. Thus, when a child sees that parents invest more time into their wants than their needs, the child learns to prefer wants to needs. While there is nothing wrong with taking a child to a water park or a shopping mall, a parent needs to make sure that meeting needs is taught as a priority of life, not as an option in life.

If we fail to teach this generation wealth-building techniques, then we will enslave the next two generations. The new type of slavery will not be based upon skin color, but rather upon a person's ability to generate capital in a capitalistic society. For example, gasoline stations set their fuel prices for the purpose of keeping certain groups out of specific neighborhoods. Housing is priced higher in certain neighborhoods that have the same floor plans—in order to keep a select group out of those neighborhoods. It is our duty to help children understand that money is not evil. However, a person with an unclean heart can use money for evil purposes (see 1 Timothy 6:10).

These are some tips for training a child to develop a mindset for wealth building:

- Do not give babies things that they do not need.

- Help your child to feel good about him- or herself without the accumulation of unnecessary things.

- Teach your child priorities.

- Teach your child the value of money as it relates to spending and saving.

- Teach your child how debt robs people of their purchasing power.

- Teach your child how to tithe and save money.

- Challenge your child to gather pennies and open a savings account in his or her name as the funds increase.

Every child can learn wealth building by gathering pennies. A penny is a dollar minus ninety-nine "friends."

DISCUSSION QUESTIONS

1. What are the first steps in teaching a Christian child how to build wealth?

2. In a capitalist society, what will be the determining signs of slavery in the future?

3. Why is it imperative for the church to participate in the training of wealth building?

6

METHODOLOGY FOR BUILDING WEALTH
WITH A PENNY

Building wealth is not an easy task—but it is possible for every free, rational person to build wealth. Therefore, it is important to have laws that protect people's right to own properties. Even though this book was written to delineate wealth-building techniques and their philosophies, it is important to have laws that protect people's property from the government and unscrupulous persons. Thus, wealth avails itself to a populous that lives in a free and democratic society. Other than having religious rights, the right to own property and to accumulate wealth is one undergirded by Scripture (see Numbers 36; Deuteronomy 8:17-18; 1 Kings 21; Psalm 112:3). In other words, every person should be free to worship and to enjoy the fruits of his or her labor.

One's being wealthy does not mean that he or she will have the same type or level of wealth as another wealthy person. In other words, the size of the house, number of cars, and amount of accumulated funds may vary from one wealthy person to another. What each wealthy person has in common with another is that there is an abundance of something. Thus, an individual's lifestyle is the key to building and determining wealth. In other words, a person will never build wealth in living like or having the same income as his or her neighbor.

It is unfortunate that the world defines wealth based upon greed and the excessive accumulation of things not needed or used. For example, what is the purpose of one's having a yacht that requires millions of dollars to maintain yet he or she rarely (if ever) uses? What is the purpose of one's having ten cars in his or her garage, when he or she has a chauffeur who drives him or her around in the company limousine? What is the purpose of one's having a gold lavatory—will it add years to his or her life? To own these types of lavish things is to live an excessive lifestyle. But it is one's possessing these material things that affords him or her the status of "wealthy" (by the world's standards). Thus, the world's model keeps most people from developing *biblical* wealth—which is to live an abundant life, not be excessively greedy.

As a person seeks to build wealth, it is important for him or her to know that abundance is not achieved at the same time. For example, some people may gain financial wealth in their thirties, while for others this status may not come to fruition until they are in their sixties. Thus, the capacity to build wealth is not the same for every person or family. Yet, every person and family has the capacity to build wealth. Every person and family has within its grasp the potential to build wealth. Therefore, this book explores the power of the penny as the foundation to build wealth. The penny has unrealized potentials. The penny helps people to understand that building wealth is a process that requires commitment, consistency, a goal, and dedication. Building wealth with a penny is not a gimmick—it is a *fact*. Oil companies and utility companies have relied on pennies to make billions of dollars for years. If these companies see the value of the penny, then it is time for ordinary people to pick up their pennies and claim their destinies.

The following information is a rundown of the subsequent charts, which serve to outline how to build wealth with a penny. The charts will help you to identify your capacity to build wealth, and they will offer other mean tests to help you to assess your position as you accumulate your wealth.

CHART #1

This chart shows how much you can save by doubling a penny each day. As you study the chart, you will notice that most people can save at least $10.24 in eleven days. If this pattern is repeated every eleven days for forty years, then a person will have saved $13,516.80. If a five-year-old child repeated this pattern until the age of 70, then the child will have saved $21,964.80. The more days that you double a penny, the greater is the saving outcome. However, to make the concept work, it will require a journal. You will need to make notes about what you can do that will increase your ability to double a penny beyond eleven days. The question has to be asked, "What am I buying that I can do without?" Wealth building is a discipline that demands sacrifice. For example, let's just say that every Saturday you spend at least $40 on a meal. If you decide to eliminate two of your Saturday meals, then you could put $80 toward your saving—toward doubling your penny. The sacrifice would amount to your having doubled the penny at the fourteen-day mark—which is $81.92. If you were to repeat this pattern for forty years, then you will have saved $85,196.80. The concept of building wealth by doubling a penny allows every person an opportunity to gain wealth, regardless of his or her social status. Thus, it requires the same qualities from every person: consistency, commitment, and dedication.

CHART #2

This chart shows how much you can save by doubling a penny each week. Doubling the penny every week instead of each day gives a person more latitude to find something that can be eliminated or adjusted. The principle is the same. And though the initial accumulation is less, in theory, the number of weeks that the effort is made to double a penny should increase. For example, eighteen weeks are approximately four months. The average person could reach a capacity of eighteen weeks rather than eighteen days, which is $1310. *Capacity,* in this regard, is defined as the number of days, weeks, or months in which an individual can double the penny. In other words, if one can double a penny for eighteen weeks—and repeat the same—then eighteen weeks is his or her capacity. Thus, to achieve an eighteen-week capacity requires a person to make a $325-per-month adjustment in spending. People who can double a penny for twenty weeks will have saved $5,242.88. Fifty-two weeks divided by twenty weeks equals 2.6 (so let's just round it to 2). Therefore, the pattern can be repeated twice per year, which is a total of $10,484.96. Assuming that a person could repeat this pattern for forty years, a person will have saved $419,398.40. The object of doubling a penny is to challenge a person to change his or her lifestyle in order to build wealth. Thus, the concept is to change the mindset from *spending* at will to *saving* at will.

CHART #3

This chart shows how much a person can save—provided he or she doubles a penny for eleven days and uses it as the foundation to double its value in months. Time and money go together. The more time a person has to grow money, the greater is the outcome. However, a daily or weekly paradigm would not afford an older person (with fewer years in which to accumulate funds) the time to make the needed adjustments. For example, take a person who is sixty-five years of age, with a house note and other bills equaling $4300, and an income of $5200 per month. Moreover, the person is in good health and intends to work until seventy years of age. Now, if the person could sell his or her house, pay cash for a smaller house, and liquidate $2500 consumer debt, then that same person could have $3400.00 per month to put toward saving. However, if the person did not adjust financial conditions, then he or she would only have available $900 per month for saving. Assuming that the person adjusted financial conditions and used chart #3 to double his or her funds, this would mean that he or she would have the resources to save a minimum of $24,500 in one year—and in ten years, he or she could have $245,000. This amount of funds is more than four times greater than the average nest egg of a person retiring between the ages of 65-75.

CHART #4

This chart looks at how much money can be saved by doubling a penny per *day*, allowing the potential saver to see the outcome of the chosen capacity in years. For example, if the potential saver chooses fourteen days as the capacity amount ($81.92), then the amount can be repeated twenty-six times within a year. Therefore, if the saver committed to thirty years, then he or she would have approximately $64,000 (plus interest) at the end of thirty years.

CHART #5

This chart looks at how much money can be saved by doubling a penny per *week*, allowing the potential saver to see the outcome of the chosen capacity in years. For example, if the potential saver chooses fifteen weeks as the capacity amount ($163.84), then the amount can be repeated three times within a year. Its outcome would be less than the amount if it were tracked by day. However, this might be a comfort level at which to start. It is important to use a journal to track your ability to make sacrificial changes in your budget that will allow for more of your income to be put toward saving. Therefore, if the saver committed to thirty years, then he or she would have approximately $15,000 (plus interest) at the end of thirty years.

CHART #6

This chart looks at how much money can be saved by doubling a penny per *month*. The chart is based upon the assumption that the potential saver doubles a penny for eleven days. The amount doubled in the first eleven days is the starting point for saving. Therefore, the first month starts with $10.24 rather than one cent. The monthly paradigm produces the greatest return for the average person. It allows the average person to make the greatest adjustment to the family budget while experiencing the least amount of stress. In addition, this paradigm is ideal for an older person who has a greater need for accumulated funds with the least amount time in which to achieve the desired goal. For example, at the end of ten months, the saver would have $5,242.88. In thirty years, the potential saver would have $157,286.40 (plus interest). For the potential saver to achieve this objective would require him or her to save an average of $524 per month.

CHART #7

This chart looks at the average salary in a forty-year span and works under the assumption that 10 percent is saved and 10 percent is given as tithes. The amount saved is also the amount given for tithing. In other words, God expects us to pay ourselves as we honor Him with a tithe. One of the most unfortunate occurrences in most churches lies in their teaching tithing as a means to build wealth.

It is taught that the tithe is an earned dollar, not a spendable dollar. In other words, it is asserted that a percentage of the dollar does not belong to the earner. In addition, it teaches that a percentage of earned dollars should be placed in a storehouse. A *storehouse* is a place where something is kept until it is needed. Thus, a person who tithes understands that a percentage of every earned dollar should be stored for future needs. This is what we call saving. If a percentage of an earned dollar is going into God's storehouse (local church) and into personal saving, it means that the earner cannot live on 100 percent of the earned dollar. Thus, the concept of tithing teaches that a percentage less than 100 percent is available for the family budget. In truth, every family should strive to live on 75 percent of every earned dollar. This formula would allow a family to have a "5-percent-rainy-day fund" in place for emergencies.

If a person truly adhered to the concepts of this chart, then he or she could produce a life of abundance and financial freedom.

Chart #1

LIVING A LIFESTYLE THAT PRODUCES WEALTH

DAY	AMOUNT	DOUBLE	TOTAL
1	$.01		$.01
2	$.01	$.02	$.02
3	$.02	$.02	$.04
4	$.04	$.04	$.08
5	$.08	$.08	$.16
6	$.16	$.16	$.32
7	$.32	$.32	$.64
8	$.64	$.64	$1.28
9	$1.28	$1.28	$2.56
10	$2.56	$2.56	$5.12
11	$5.12	$5.12	$10.24
12	$10.24	$10.24	$20.48
13	$20.48	$20.48	$40.96
14	$40.96	$40.96	$81.92
15	$81.92	$81.92	$163.84
16	$163.92	$163.92	$327.68
17	$327.68	$327.68	$655.36
18	$655.36	$655.36	$1,310.72
19	$1,310.72	$1,310.72	$2,621.44
20	$2,621.44	$2,621.44	$5,242.88

Chart #2

LIVING A LIFESTYLE THAT PRODUCES WEALTH

WEEK	AMOUNT	ADD	TOTAL
1	$.01		$.01
2	$.01	$.02	$.02
3	$.02	$.02	$.04
4	$.04	$.04	$.08
5	$.08	$.08	$.16
6	$.16	$.16	$.32
7	$.32	$.32	$.64
8	$.64	$.64	$1.28
9	$1.28	$1.28	$2.56
10	$2.56	$2.56	$5.12
11	$5.12	$5.12	$10.24
12	$10.24	$10.24	$20.48
13	$20.48	$20.48	$40.96
14	$40.96	$40.96	$81.92
15	$81.92	$81.92	$163.84
16	$163.92	$163.92	$327.68
17	$327.68	$327.68	$655.36
18	$655.36	$655.36	$1,310.72
19	$1,310.72	$1,310.72	$2,621.44
20	$2,621.44	$2,621.44	$5,242.88

Chart #3

LIVING A LIFESTYLE THAT PRODUCES WEALTH

MONTH	ADD	TOTAL
1	$10.24	$10.24
2	$10.24	$20.48
3	$20.48	$40.96
4	$40.96	$81.92
5	$81.92	$163.84
6	$163.84	$327.68
7	$327.68	$655.36
8	$655.36	$1,310.72
9	$1,310.72	$2,621.44
10	$2,621.44	$5,242.88
11	$5,242.88	$10,485.76
12	$10,485.76	$20,971.52

Chart #4

LIVING A LIFESTYLE THAT PRODUCES WEALTH

CAPACITY AND RESULTS

D	C/M	C/A	5 YRS.	10 YRS.	20 YRS.	30 YRS.
10	36	$5.12	$922	$1,840	$3,686	$5,530
11	33	$10.24	$1,690	$3,379	$6,758	$10,138
12	30	$20.48	$3,072	$6,144	$12,288	$18,432
14	26	$81.92	$10,650	$21,299	$42,598	$63,898
15	24	$163.84	$19,660	$39,322	$78,643	$117,965
16	22	$327.68	$36,045	$72,090	$144,179	$216,269
20	18	$5,242.88	$471,858	$943,718	$1,887,437	$28,311,552

D = DAYS

C/M = CAPACITY MULTIPLIER (365-10) = 36x$5.12x5 = $922

C/A = CAPACITY AMOUNT

Chart #5

LIVING A LIFESTYLE THAT PRODUCES WEALTH

CAPACITY AND RESULTS

WKS.	C/M	C/A	5 YRS.	10 YRS.	20 YRS.	30 YRS.
10	5	$5.12	$128	$256	$512	$768
15	3	$163.84	$2,458	$4,915	$9,830	$14,746
20	2	$5,242.88	$52,429	$104,858	$209,715	$314,573
21	2	$10,485.76	$104,858	$209,715	$419,430	$629,146

WKS. = WEEKS

C/M = CAPACITY MULTIPLIER (52-10) = 5x$5.12x5 = $128

C/A = CAPACITY AMOUNT

Chart #6

LIVING A LIFESTYLE THAT PRODUCES WEALTH

CAPACITY AND RESULTS

M	C/M	C/A	5 YRS.	10 YRS.	20 YRS.	30 YRS.
5	2	$163.84	$1,638.40	$3,276.80	$6,553.60	$9,830.40
8	1	$1,310.72	$6,553.60	$13,017.20	$26,214.40	$39,321.60
10	1	$5,242.88	$26,214.40	$52,428.80	$104,857.60	$157,286.40
12	1	$20,971.52	$104,857.60	$209,715.20	$419,430.40	$629,145.60

M = MONTHS

C/M = CAPACITY MULTIPLIER (12-5) = 2X$163.84X5 = $1638.40

C/A = CAPACITY AMOUNT

Chart #7

TITHING/SAVING

A/SALARY	40 YRS./INCOME	10 YRS.	20 YRS.	30 YRS.	40 YRS.
$15,000	$600,000	$15,000	$30,000	$45,000	$60,000
$25,000	$1,000,000	$25,000	$50,000	$75,000	$100,000
$35,000	$1,400,000	$35,000	$70,000	$105,000	$140,000
$45,000	$1,800,000	$45,000	$90,000	$135,000	$180,000
$55,000	$2,200,000	$55,000	$110,000	$165,000	$220,000
$65,000	$2,600,000	$65,000	$130,000	$195,000	$260,000
$75,000	$3,000,000	$75,000	$150,000	$225,000	$300,000
$85,000	$3,400,000	$85,000	$170,000	$255,000	$340,000
$95,000	$3,800,000	$95,000	$190,000	$285,000	$380,000
$100,000	$4,000,000	$100,000	$200,000	$300,000	$400,000

A/Salary = Average salary over forty years

The second column is the total amount of money earned over forty years (based upon an average salary).

*This chart looks at the average salary for forty years and makes the assumption that 10 percent of the salary is saved, and 10 percent is given as tithes. The amount saved is also the amount given as tithes. This chart gives a person a visual of the amount of money to be earned and the amount of money to be saved over a forty-year span. In other words, God expects us to pay ourselves as we honor Him with a tithe (refer to 1 Corinthians 9:10). The purpose of one's tithing is to build wealth as he or she honors God.

SAVING

Now it is time to get started. Find an empty envelope and write on it the number days that you can double a penny. At the end of each term (the number of days), repeat it, and deposit your funds into a savings account. You should open a new savings account. For example, if you can double a penny for fourteen (14) days, then this is your capacity. Thus, you are to repeat it every fourteen days. As your funds grow in a regular savings account, consider moving some of your funds to a higher fixed investment, such as a Certificate of Deposit.

Finally, your repeating your pattern for one year will save you approximately $2,130. So use your journal to find means to increase your capacity. You will notice that your lifestyle has been revolutionized when you find yourself going to the bank to make your deposits.

Illustration

DAY
1 2 3 4 5 6 7 8 9 10 11 12 13 14
TO THE BANK

Journal

The success of the penny model requires utilization of a daily journal. The art of building wealth, according to lifestyle preference, lies in an individual's being challenged to take daily actions in order to meet that goal. One of the first questions that one should ask him- or herself is this: "Am I ready to commitment to wealth building, not spending to appear wealthy?" In other words, "Am I working to build wealth, or am I working to spend money on things that give the appearance of wealth?" Too many people work to buy things and not to save funds to build wealth. Thus, most working people would not have a retirement account if it were not for their employers' forcing them to save.

A budget has to be set or real sacrifices have to be made in order to develop the capacity to save. For example, say you have a habit of eating seafood at a particular food establishment every Friday with a predetermined amount of funds—or you buy your groceries without a meal menu to follow. Well, if you buy your groceries with a meal menu in mind, you can save money; and these savings can be used to build your capacity (the number of days, weeks, or months in which you can double a penny). A journal will allow you to see ahead of each day—just make a note about the decisions that you made in order to have funds available to double your effort (before the funds were needed). Assess what you did on day 1 or day 5 to have funds in place to double day 11, which is $10.24. Knowing what you did will allow you to repeat your pattern, and to make an adjustment in certain areas (if needed).

Recording in the journal will help you to determine which method (by days, weeks, or months) will work best for you. An individual will need to start at a comfortable level and also be willing to change—as lifestyle adjustments are made to maximize potential savings.

PERSONAL JOURNAL

A CAPACITY PLANNER FOR A TWELVE-DAY OR TWELVE-WEEK PATTERN

DAY/WK 1 _____

DAY/WK 2 _____

DAY/WK 3 _____

DAY/WK 4 _____

DAY/WK 5 _____

DAY/WK 6 _____

DAY/WK 7 _____

DAY/WK 8 _____

DAY/WK 9 _____

DAY/WK 10 _____

DAY/WK 11 _____

DAY/WK 12 _____

A CAPACITY PLANNER FOR A THIRTEEN-DAY OR THIRTEEN-WEEK PATTERN

DAY/WK 1 _____

DAY/WK 2 _____

DAY/WK 3 _____

DAY/WK 4 _____

DAY/WK 5 _____

DAY/WK 6 _____

DAY/WK 7 _____

DAY/WK 8 _____

DAY/WK 9 _____

DAY/WK 10 _____

DAY/WK 11 _____

DAY/WK 12 _____

DAY/WK 13 _____

A CAPACITY PLANNER FOR A FOURTEEN-DAY OR FOURTEEN-WEEK PATTERN

DAY/WK 1 _____

DAY/WK 2 _____

DAY/WK 3 _____

DAY/WK 4 _____

DAY/WK 5 _____

DAY/WK 6 _____

DAY/WK 7 _____

DAY/WK 8 _____

DAY/WK 9 _____

DAY/WK 10 _____

DAY/WK 11 _____

DAY/WK 12 _____

DAY/WK 13 _____

DAY/WK 14 _____

A CAPACITY PLANNER FOR A FIFTEEN-DAY OR FIFTEEN-WEEK PATTERN

DAY/WK 1 _____

DAY/WK 2 _____

DAY/WK 3 _____

DAY/WK 4 _____

DAY/WK 5 _____

DAY/WK 6 _____

DAY/WK 7 _____

DAY/WK 8 _____

DAY/WK 9 _____

DAY/WK 10 _____

DAY/WK 11 _____

DAY/WK 12 _____

DAY/WK 13 _____

DAY/WK 14 _____

DAY/WK 15 _____

A CAPACITY PLANNER FOR A SIXTEEN-DAY OR SIXTEEN-WEEK PATTERN

DAY/WK 1 _____

DAY/WK 2 _____

DAY/WK 3 _____

DAY/WK 4 _____

DAY/WK 5 _____

DAY/WK 6 _____

DAY/WK 7 _____

DAY/WK 8 _____

DAY/WK 9 _____

DAY/WK 10 _____

DAY/WK 11 _____

DAY/WK 12 _____

DAY/WK 13 _____

DAY/WK 14 _____

DAY/WK 15 _____

DAY/WK 16 _____

A CAPACITY PLANNER FOR A SEVENTEEN-DAY OR SEVENTEEN-WEEK PATTERN

DAY/WK 1 _____

DAY/WK 2 _____

DAY/WK 3 _____

DAY/WK 4 _____

DAY/WK 5 _____

DAY/WK 6 _____

DAY/WK 7 _____

DAY/WK 8 _____

DAY/WK 9 _____

DAY/WK 10 _____

DAY/WK 11 _____

DAY/WK 12 _____

DAY/WK 13 _____

DAY/WK 14 _____

DAY/WK 15 _____

DAY/WK 16 _____

DAY/WK 17 _____

A CAPACITY PLANNER FOR AN EIGHTEEN-DAY OR EIGHTEEN-WEEK PATTERN

DAY/WK 1 _____

DAY/WK 2 _____

DAY/WK 3 _____

DAY/WK 4 _____

DAY/WK 5 _____

DAY/WK 6 _____

DAY/WK 7 _____

DAY/WK 8 _____

DAY/WK 9 _____

DAY/WK 10 _____

DAY/WK 11 _____

DAY/WK 12 _____

DAY/WK 13 _____

DAY/WK 14 _____

DAY/WK 15 _____

DAY/WK 16 _____

DAY/WK 17 _____

DAY/WK 18 _____

A CAPACITY PLANNER FOR A NINETEEN-DAY OR NINETEEN-WEEK PATTERN

DAY/WK 1 _____

DAY/WK 2 _____

DAY/WK 3 _____

DAY/WK 4 _____

DAY/WK 5 _____

DAY/WK 6 _____

DAY/WK 7 _____

DAY/WK 8 _____

DAY/WK 9 _____

DAY/WK 10 _____

DAY/WK 11 _____

DAY/WK 12 _____

DAY/WK 13 _____

DAY/WK 14 _____

DAY/WK 15 _____

DAY/WK 16 _____

DAY/WK 17 _____

DAY/WK 18 _____

DAY/WK 19 _____

A CAPACITY PLANNER FOR A TWENTY-DAY OR TWENTY-WEEK PATTERN

DAY/WK 1 _____

DAY/WK 2 _____

DAY/WK 3 _____

DAY/WK 4 _____

DAY/WK 5 _____

DAY/WK 6 _____

DAY/WK 7 _____

DAY/WK 8 _____

DAY/WK 9 _____

DAY/WK 10 _____

DAY/WK 11 _____

DAY/WK 12 _____

DAY/WK 13 _____

DAY/WK 14 _____

DAY/WK 15 _____

DAY/WK 16 _____

DAY/WK 17 _____

DAY/WK 18 _____

DAY/WK 19 _____

DAY/WK 20 _____

A CAPACITY PLANNER FOR A TWENTY-ONE-DAY OR TWENTY-ONE-WEEK PATTERN

DAY/WK 1 _____

DAY/WK 2 _____

DAY/WK 3 _____

DAY/WK 4 _____

DAY/WK 5 _____

DAY/WK 6 _____

DAY/WK 7 _____

DAY/WK 8 _____

DAY/WK 9 _____

DAY/WK 10 _____

DAY/WK 11 _____

DAY/WK 12 _____

DAY/WK 13 _____

DAY/WK 14 _____

DAY/WK 15 _____

DAY/WK 16 _____

DAY/WK 17 _____

DAY/WK 18 _____

DAY/WK 19 _____

DAY/WK 20 _____

DAY/WK 21 _____

A CAPACITY PLANNER FOR A TWELVE-MONTH PATTERN

MONTH 1 _____

MONTH 2 _____

MONTH 3 _____

MONTH 4 _____

MONTH 5 _____

MONTH 6 _____

MONTH 7 _____

MONTH 8 _____

MONTH 9 _____

MONTH 10 _____

MONTH 11 _____

MONTH 12 _____

APPENDIX

How to Use This Book for Group Study

Even though this book was written to help people build wealth, it is an excellent book for teaching people how to live a debt-free lifestyle. Living debt-free is possible. Thus, this book helps people to see how debt robs persons of their potential to live comfortably in their retirement years, and in times of economic hardships. As long as this world exists, there will be economic hardship—personally, locally, and globally. This is why it is wise to adhere to the Scriptures and to apply them, both literally and practically. The Scriptures teach that we are to save money for the hard times (see Genesis 41:28-36).

First, as the leader (or facilitator) of the study, take time to read each chapter for discussion. It is important to understand the philosophy of the model. As you read and understand each chapter, you may challenge the group to find additional Scripture passages that deal with wealth building, or other information that gives insight into the diversity of money management. Second, make plans to read one chapter at each group session (making the sessions either formal or informal). A formal session would *require* the group to have a facilitator. This person could be the pastor, the pastor's appointee, or a person who has knowledge of finances. If the group is not affiliated with a church, then the facilitator needs to be a person who has experience in the financial arena. The facilitator should engage the participants in some type of regular study routine for comprehension purposes. This approach allows persons to develop a hands-on technique, as they acquire the philosophy—in the hope of transitioning into applying the practicality of wealth building.

In addition, the book can be used for Bible study. The twenty-first-century church members face new challenges that require them to go beyond the rudimental foundation of Christianity (see Hebrews 6:1-3). In other words, the church has to meet more than the spiritual needs of its parishioners. Too often, when the church fails to minister to the physical needs of its parishioners, these persons then seek unholy and ungodly methods to meet that which should have been addressed with biblical principles and concepts. The church should not be intimidated when it comes to teaching

Christians how to build wealth. Far too many Christians believe that all they need to do is name it and claim it. If building wealth were that easy, then every Christian would be wealthy—by desire only. God wants us to be wealthy and prosperous. However, there is not anything magical about wealth or prosperity. Wealth comes by dedication, consistency, commitment, and, for Christians, obedience to God's principles that deal with wealth.

Third, take time to study the charts. The charts help the potential saver to find the right starting point. Reading the book without starting the process is like having medicine in the medicine cabinet and not taking it. There is no perfect method to building wealth. Every person has to start somewhere with a particular plan and make adjustments—while staying committed to the objective of building wealth. What makes this model unique is that it allows persons with no capital to build capital. In addition, the charts provide outlines that allow persons to see the particular model's capacity outcomes.

Fourth, chart #7 allows one to see the average earned income over forty years of work, while at the same time reflecting on funds that should have been saved and tithed. This is an excellent tool in helping Christians to see the practicality of tithing. Sometimes people need to see an example of possible outcomes before committing to truth. Tithing is God's standard for our honoring Him as the provider of our resources; but this practice yields more than our honoring God—it teaches the core principle of wealth building.

Fifth, the book can be used for teaching children how to save and the purpose for saving. Chart #1 serves to be encouragement to children to save pennies while at the same time teaching them the source of wealth. It allows the child to achieve a goal that is obtainable, realistic, and practical. Once a child has gathered at least $100 in pennies, he or she can then go to the bank and open a savings account or buy a government bond.

Finally, this is an excellent book for families. Often quoted is the adage, "The family that prays together stays together." It can also be said, "The family that *plans* together *grows* together." One of the leading causes of frustration and confusion in the family is the lack of money or the misuse of money. *Grace* can bring a family together in building wealth that is consistent with biblical principles, thereby creating tranquility among individual family members.

Miscellaneous Tips

Nothing in life is easy. Life has its way of taming the most ambitious person. However, some persons manage to take control of their lives and fulfill their true destinies in life. The answer to this dilemma is found in Scripture and the wisdom of living. A wise man once said, "He that will control others must first control him- or herself." Jesus said, "He that will follow me must first deny himself" (see Matthew 16:24). Thus, the real secret to wealth building is having the ability to deny self. The greatest enemy of every person is his/her ego. The ego masquerades as a protector, a lover, and an advisor. The ego is adept at disguising its true intent. The ego lusts for attention and affection. Thus, if persons are to be successful in wealth building, then they must be willing to do battle with their egos. Thus, I have listed several tips that will help people to do battle with their egos:

1. Be happy for others without wanting to share the stage.

2. Take time to discover those things that are closest to you.

3. Focus on needs that have a long-term result rather than a short-term gratification.

4. Seek to understand the influence of wealth, not its consumption power.

5. Seek to live comfortably, rather than live as a celebrity.

6. Learn to wait in order to prepare for tomorrow's opportunities.

7. Know that your ownership of expensive things does not make you wealthy.

8. Make saving a priority of life rather than a notion of life.

9. Seek ways to make life better for others.

10. Find ways to give back to those who have helped you.

11. Live life without fear of not enjoying the fruits of your earthly labors.

12. Honor God cheerfully and wholeheartedly with your earthly possessions.

The Family Budget

MONTHLY INCOME

    PRIMARY   _____

    SECONDARY   _____

    OTHER   _____

    TOTAL   _____

MONTHLY HOUSEHOLD EXPENSES

    RENT/MORTAGE   _____

    SECOND MORTAGE _____

    UTILITIES

        ELECTRIC   _____

        GAS   _____

        SOLAR   _____

        WATER/SEWAGE _____

        TRASH DISPOSAL _____

    TRANSPORTATION

    CAR PAYMENTS   _____

    PUBLIC   _____

    GASOLINE   _____

COMMUNICATION

    LAND PHONE   _____

    CELL PHONE   _____

    INTERNET   _____

    CABLE   _____

INSURANCES

    HEALTH   _____

    LIFE   _____

    DISABILITY   _____

HOUSE _____

AUTO _____

RETIREMENT _____

MEDICAL

ANNUAL PHYSICAL _____

CO-PAYMENTS _____

DENTAL _____

EDUCATIONAL TUITION

COLLEGE _____

PRIVATE SCHOOL _____

DAYCARE _____

ADULT CARE _____

SCHOOL SUPPLIES _____

FOOD

GROCERIES _____

SCHOOL LUNCHES _____

WORK LUNCHES _____

FAMILY OUTINGS _____

CLOTHING

HUSBAND _____

WIFE _____

CHILDREN _____

COMSUMER DEBT

CREDIT CARDS _____

OTHER _____

PERSONAL GROOMING

HAIRCUTS _____

HAIR STYLING _____

OTHER _____

ENTERTAINMENT
      MOVIES   _____
      THEATER   _____
      BOOKS   _____
      NEWSPAPERS   _____
      MAGAZINES   _____
      VACATION   _____

PROFESSIONAL FEES
      CLUBS   _____
      BANKING   _____
      OTHER   _____

CHARITY
      TITHES (10 PERCENT)   _____
      OTHER   _____

SAVING
      EMERGENCY (5 PERCENT)   _____
      COLLEGE   _____
      PERSONAL   _____

MISCELLANEOUS
      _____

TOTAL MONTHLY HOUSEHOLD EXPENSES

_____

NET INCOME AFTER EXPENSES   _____

NOTE:
TITHES ARE 10 PERCENT OF INCOME
EMERGENCY SAVINGS SHOULD BE AT LEAST 5 PERCENT OF INCOME
OTHER SAVINGS SHOULD EQUAL TO 10 PERCENT OF INCOME
RETIREMENT SAVINGS are usually deducted from gross income. If retirement savings is not deducted from gross income, then it should be at least 3 percent of earned income.

REFERENCES

Alcorn, Randy. *Managing God's Money*. Carol Stream, Tyndale House Publisher, Incorporated.

Bell, Matt. *Money & Marriage*. Colorado Springs, NavPress.

Blue, Ron and Jeremy White, CPA. *Surviving Financial Meltdown*. Carol Stream, Tyndale House Publisher, Incorporated.

Burkett, Larry. *Debt-free Living*. Chicago, Moody Press.

Burkett, Larry and Randy Southern. *The World's Greatest Guide to Finances*. Chicago, Northfield Publishing.

Hunt, Mary. *Can I Pay My Credit Card Bill With a Credit Card?* California, DPL Press.

Ramsey, Dave. *The Financial Planner*. New York, Penguin Books.

WEB SITES

http://www.gospel.com/topics/finances

http://finance.yahoo.com/personal-finance

http://www.kiplinger.com

http://en.wikipedia.org/wiki/Finance

http://www.suzeorman.com

OTHER BOOKS BY THE AUTHOR

Prophetic Building (A Nightmare or Vision)
Retail Price: $14.95
ISBN 0-9764174-1-3

Preparing Your Church for Pastoral Leadership
Retail Price: $9.95
ISBN 978-0-615-31874-5

Order Your Book Today!
Local Bookstores
Barnes & Noble
Amazon.com
Lowbar Online Store: http://shop.Lowbarbookstore.com

Discount Price for Bookstores and Book Club Ministries
Please e-mail for discount prices: Lowbar@comcast.net

Notes

Notes